Courageous Kids

T0009064

ANNE FRANK
WRITES WORDS OF HOPE
COURAGEOUS KID OF WORLD WAR II

by Debbie Vilardi

illustrated by Christian Papazoglakis

CAPSTONE PRESS
a capstone imprint

Published by Capstone Press, an imprint of Capstone
1710 Roe Crest Drive North Mankato, Minnesota 56003
capstonepub.com

Library of Congress Cataloging-in-Publication Data is available on the Library of Congress website.
ISBN: 9781666334197 (hardcover)
ISBN: 9781666334227 (paperback)
ISBN: 9781666334210 (ebook PDF)

Summary: In 1933, the Nazi Party rose to power in Germany. The Nazis murdered millions of Jews and other people across Europe during World War II. However, young Anne Frank and her family managed to hide from the Nazis for two years. During this time, Anne wrote about her experiences almost every day in her diary. Discover the courage of Anne and her family during one of the most horrific times in history.

EDITOR
Aaron Sautter

DESIGNER
Brann Garvey

MEDIA RESEARCHER
Morgan Walters

PRODUCTION SPECIALIST
Polly Fisher

All internet sites appearing in back matter were available and accurate when this book was sent to press.

All diary entries shown are from *The Diary of Anne Frank: The Critical Edition*, Ed. David Barnouw and Gerald van der Stroom. New York: Doubleday, 1989.

Direct quotations appear in ***bold italicized text*** on the following pages:

Page 4: from "Extracts from *Mein Kampf* by Adolf Hitler," Houghtan Mifflin, New York: Hutchinson Pub. Ltd., London, 1969. https://www.wm.edu/offices/auxiliary/osher/course-info/classnotes/fall2017/Schilling_Holocaust-Extracts-from-Mein-Kampf-Ideology.pdf

Pages 17, 22, and 29: from *The Diary of Anne Frank: The Critical Edition*, Ed. David Barnouw and Gerald van der Stroom. New York: Doubleday, 1989.

Page 26: from "D-Day as the BBC Reported It on Radio News," BBC News, June 5, 2019, https://www.bbc.com/news/av/uk-48525818.

Page 28: from "Dear Kitty," Remembering Anne Frank: Part 5, May 30, 2008, https://www.youtube.com/watch?v=AdJ-hV61x5U.

Printed in the United States 5290

TABLE OF CONTENTS

THE RISE OF NAZISM 4

UNWANTED JEWS 6

IN HIDING 10

CHANGES AND FEARS 16

1944 20

ANNE'S LASTING LEGACY 28

GLOSSARY 30

READ MORE 31

INTERNET SITES 31

INDEX 32

THE RISE OF NAZISM

After losing World War I (1914–1918), Germany owed money to many countries. Poor financial management and the Great Depression (1929–1941) made the economy even worse. These hardships led to the rise of the Nazi Party, led by Adolf Hitler.

The Nazi Party became very popular. Hitler became chancellor of Germany on January 30, 1933 and declared himself to be the country's *Führer*, or leader, in 1934.

Hitler and the Nazis blamed Jewish people for many of the country's problems. In 1924, Hitler had written, "*I believe that . . . by defending myself against the Jew, I am fighting for the work of the Lord.*" He soon began making anti-Semitic laws.

Soon people were told not to shop in Jewish stores or to see Jewish doctors or lawyers. Laws were passed to keep Jews from having many jobs. Jewish children were forced to go to separate schools.

Deutsche! Wehrt Euch! kauft nicht bei Juden

I never attend Jewish services. I'm a veteran and a native German. But now I'm not allowed to earn a living!

Jews were not the only group Hitler mistreated. He also imprisoned his political enemies in work camps, called concentration camps. Later, the Nazis built other camps that were used as killing centers.

Many Jewish families left Germany because they thought life for Jews would get even worse. The Franks were one of those families. Otto Frank departed before his wife, Edith, and daughters, Margot and Anne.

Bye, Daddy. Write first to me and then to Margot.

Write us as soon as you can.

The Franks didn't know it then, but Anne's life and works would later become one of the world's greatest stories of courage.

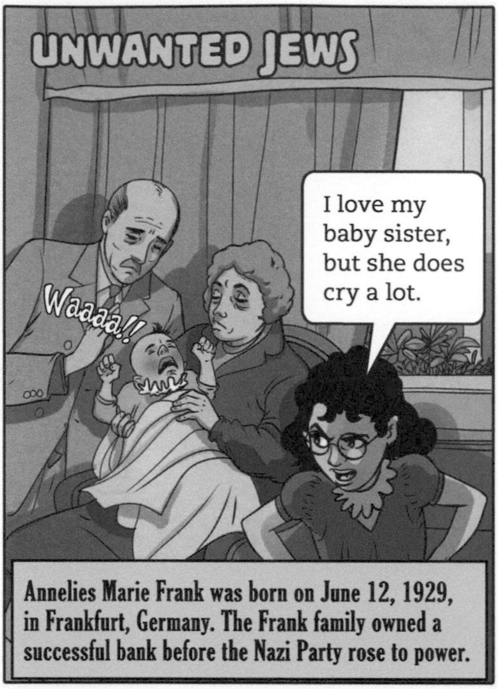
UNWANTED JEWS
Waaaa!!
I love my baby sister, but she does cry a lot.
Annelies Marie Frank was born on June 12, 1929, in Frankfurt, Germany. The Frank family owned a successful bank before the Nazi Party rose to power.

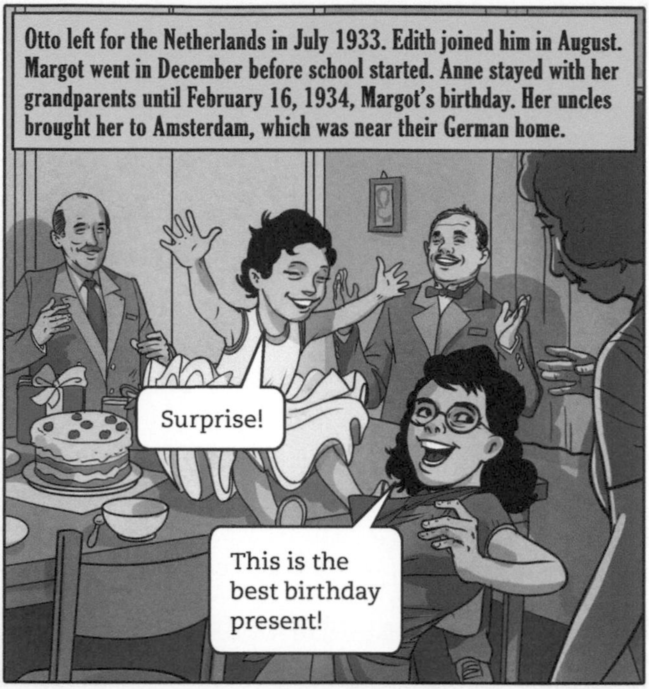
Otto left for the Netherlands in July 1933. Edith joined him in August. Margot went in December before school started. Anne stayed with her grandparents until February 16, 1934, Margot's birthday. Her uncles brought her to Amsterdam, which was near their German home.
Surprise!
This is the best birthday present!

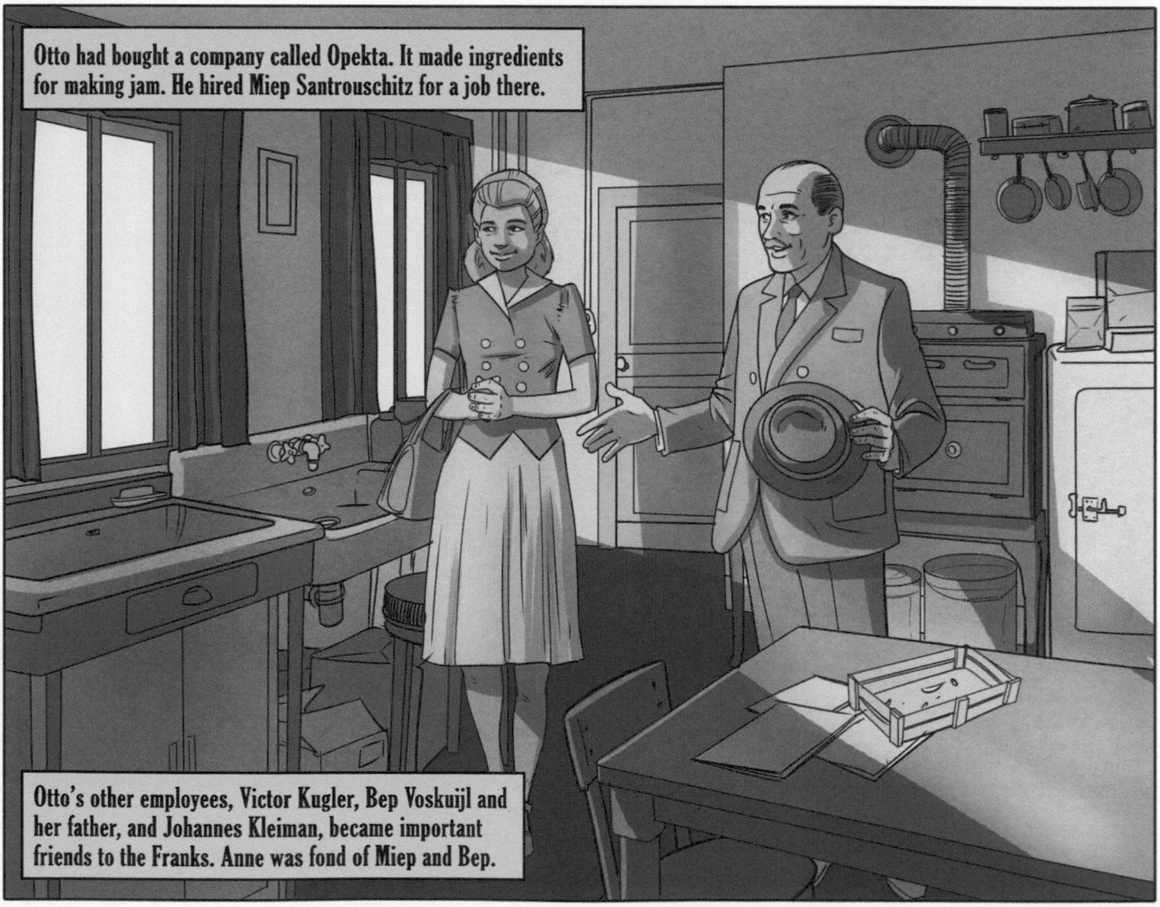
Otto had bought a company called Opekta. It made ingredients for making jam. He hired Miep Santrouschitz for a job there.
Otto's other employees, Victor Kugler, Bep Voskuijl and her father, and Johannes Kleiman, became important friends to the Franks. Anne was fond of Miep and Bep.

Anne adjusted easily to life in the Netherlands. She became friends with Dutch and German girls.

She enjoyed ice skating, swimming, reading, writing, and visiting family.

You're not the best with the scooter, but you are with jump rope. I'm better on the scooter. Let's trade.

In 1938, Hitler began sending Jews to concentration camps by the thousands. Some were allowed to leave Germany as refugees. This saved their lives.

Later, Jews weren't freed for any reason. Over 6 million died in the death camps. This mass killing is called the Holocaust (1938–1945). The Nazis also targeted the Roma, or people who had mixed Indian and European ancestry, gay people, and other groups that Hitler didn't like.

What will they do to us?

This must be all the Jews in Germany!

Why are we here?

7

On September 1, 1939, Germany attacked Poland. This marked the beginning of World War II (1939–1945). Hitler promised to respect neutral countries.

What if Hitler invades the Netherlands?

Dad says the Netherlands will be neutral like in World War I. We're safe.

But Hitler didn't keep his promise. Germany invaded the Netherlands on May 10, 1940. The Netherlands surrendered five days later.

Otto knew the Nazis had taken businesses from Jews in Germany. He believed they would do the same in the Netherlands. To protect his company, he sold Opekta to Miep and her husband.

You may not be the owner anymore . . .

. . . but you're still our boss.

Exactly right. So here are yesterday's receipts.

Many Jews were afraid and tried to escape to other countries. But countries limited how many refugees they would permit. The Franks were stuck in the Netherlands.

In October 1940, the new Nazi-controlled government in the Netherlands passed several anti-Jewish laws. Jews were forbidden to do many activities. Later, Jewish children were segregated from public schools.

It's hard to remember what is still allowed.

We can't swim, skate, or do anything.

At least we can still go to school.

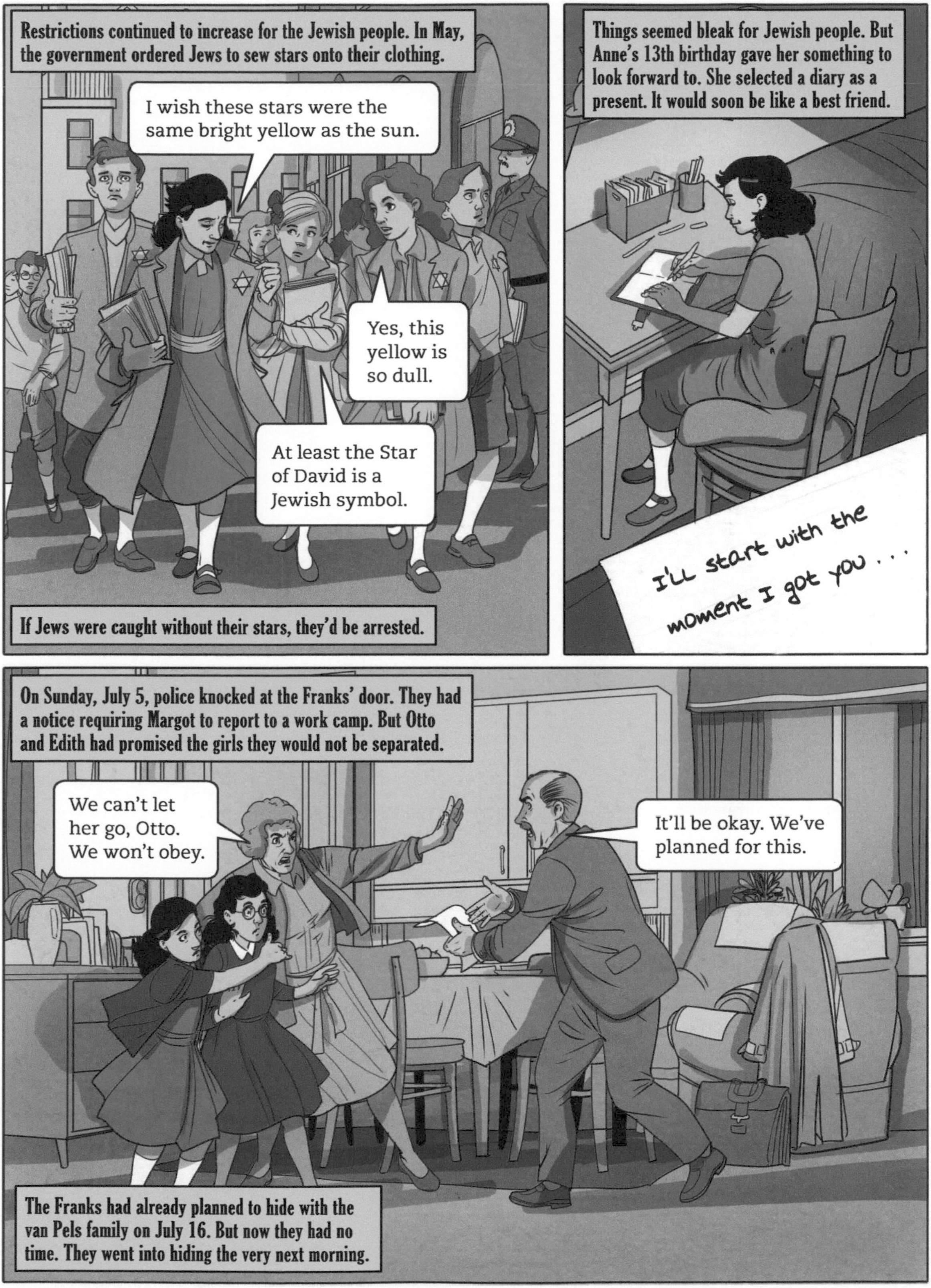
Restrictions continued to increase for the Jewish people. In May, the government ordered Jews to sew stars onto their clothing.
I wish these stars were the same bright yellow as the sun.
Yes, this yellow is so dull.
At least the Star of David is a Jewish symbol.
If Jews were caught without their stars, they'd be arrested.
Things seemed bleak for Jewish people. But Anne's 13th birthday gave her something to look forward to. She selected a diary as a present. It would soon be like a best friend.
I'll start with the moment I got you . . .
On Sunday, July 5, police knocked at the Franks' door. They had a notice requiring Margot to report to a work camp. But Otto and Edith had promised the girls they would not be separated.
We can't let her go, Otto. We won't obey.
It'll be okay. We've planned for this.
The Franks had already planned to hide with the van Pels family on July 16. But now they had no time. They went into hiding the very next morning.

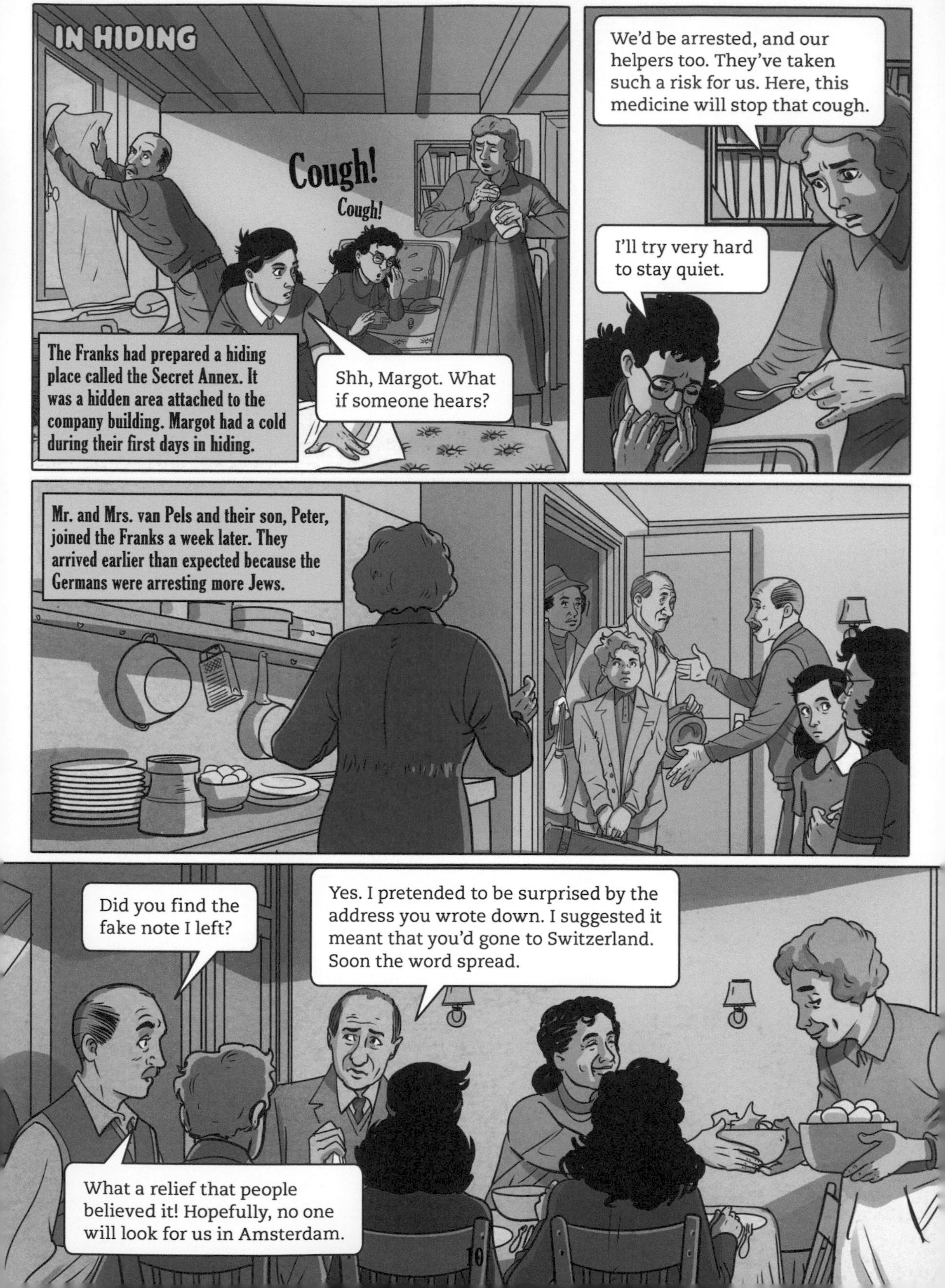
IN HIDING
Cough!
Cough!
The Franks had prepared a hiding place called the Secret Annex. It was a hidden area attached to the company building. Margot had a cold during their first days in hiding.
Shh, Margot. What if someone hears?
We'd be arrested, and our helpers too. They've taken such a risk for us. Here, this medicine will stop that cough.
I'll try very hard to stay quiet.
Mr. and Mrs. van Pels and their son, Peter, joined the Franks a week later. They arrived earlier than expected because the Germans were arresting more Jews.
Did you find the fake note I left?
Yes. I pretended to be surprised by the address you wrote down. I suggested it meant that you'd gone to Switzerland. Soon the word spread.
What a relief that people believed it! Hopefully, no one will look for us in Amsterdam.

The annex space was about the same size as a two-car garage. During work hours, the families had to be quiet so no one below would know they were there. Even running water or a flushing toilet from above might cause someone to ask questions.

Opekta company building

the Secret Annex

To hide the entrance, I could add a bookcase in front of the door.

I'd first have to remove the steps. Then we'd just need something to cover the top.

Perhaps this map could go above the door.

Perfect.

Anne was impressed by how well the bookcase hid the doorway. But her favorite thing was the daily visits from the company employees.

When will we get more books? I've finished the last two you brought.

I'm afraid you'll have to wait until Saturday.

I'm working on getting some sweaters too.

Their helpers supplied food, clothes, games, books, and writing materials. Anne used these to do her lessons and to continue her diary after filling the first one.

The families soon adjusted to daily life in the annex. They kept a schedule to make sure everyone could do their daily tasks.

August 1, 1942
We get up at 7 and line up for the bathroom, then we go upstairs to have breakfast, then comes the washing up and some sort of household chore or other.

Daily chores included removing the blackout screens from the windows and peeling potatoes. A grocer delivered sacks on business days.

September 28, 1942
The whole orphanage as we call it had to help with peeling potatoes and putting them through the grating machine.

Anne quietly read, wrote, and studied during the day while the offices and warehouse were occupied. She struggled most with math.

I don't understand this at all.

The steps are all here. Try again.

She also studied French, English, history, and a few other subjects.

After the office closed and the workers left, the families exercised and listened to the radio. Otto reviewed Opekta business. Margot and Anne helped organize the company's papers.

It's good to file these for Miep and Bep.

Yes. They do so much for us. This is a small way we can help them.

With the work done, the families took turns getting ready for bed.

Only the office kitchen had hot water. So everyone took turns to bathe once per week.

September 27, 1942
First I carry a small washtub downstairs to the large w.c.*, ... run hot water into the tub in the office kitchen, and then I go and put my feet in it, meanwhile sitting on the w.c. and start to wash myself.

* A W.C., or water closet, is another name for a bathroom or toilet.

Although the families were safely hidden, the adults often argued about the war and fair sharing. The Franks and van Pels parented their children differently. Anne was often the subject of their arguments.

If Anne won't eat vegetables, she shouldn't have potatoes.

Anne, here. Have your potatoes first.

If Anne were my child, she'd eat vegetables.

Edith loved Anne, but they didn't always get along. On October 2, 1942, they had a fight that drove them both to tears.

You're so much nicer, Papa. I love you more.

You'll get over that.

I won't.

Perhaps if you help her sometimes, you may grow to understand one another.

Margot often took their mother's side. Anne was sometimes jealous of Margot and Edith's relationship. Margot was rarely yelled at by anyone.

Maybe you should stop being such a goody-goody, Margot.

I'll try.

14

Despite the arguments, there were cheery moments in the annex. The helpers joined the families to celebrate birthdays, Jewish holidays, and Christian holidays. Everyone laughed and told jokes.

Tonight, I give thanks to all of you—for safety, good food, and good friends.

However, visits from the helpers weren't always fun. They sometimes brought shocking news about how Jews were being treated.

October 3, 1942
This morning Miep told us that last night they were dragging Jews from house after house again in South Amsterdam. Horrible. God knows which of our acquaintances are left.

CHANGES AND FEARS

The families also feared for their own safety. Any visitor to the offices might hear them or notice if something was out of place.

The plumber will be here in the morning to fix some pipes. You must stay extra quiet.

We'll be like mice.

At night, sirens warned of Allied planes flying overhead. The sounds of gunfire echoed across the sky. Terrified, Anne often slept in her father's bed for comfort.

I feel safer here with Papa.

The families had a great scare in October 1942. The helpers forgot to warn them that a carpenter would be coming to fix the door to the landing.

BANG BANG BANG BANG

I hear something.

It sounds like hammering.

During a quick break, the carpenter rattled the secret bookcase door. Anne was terrified. She imagined that they'd all be captured and killed. An hour later, she was still shaking.

As the Nazis' treatment of Jews grew worse, the families invited Fritz Pfeffer to join them in their hiding place. When he arrived on November 16, 1942, Anne read him a list of "rules" to follow.

. . . Lunch, not very big. 1:15—1:45 p.m. Dinner, cold and/or hot, no fixed time . . .

Anne's humorous reading of the rules helped Pfeffer adjust to his new situation.

Pfeffer told the families about friends who'd been taken by the Nazis. Anne felt helpless, but she understood . . .

It won't do us any good or help those outside to go on being as gloomy as we are.

Margot moved into her parents' room, which left Anne to share a space with Pfeffer. Anne was happy to help him, but he often scolded her.

You need to pile your things neatly on the table. And don't turn over in your sleep . . .

. . . it awakens me.

He also complained to Edith about Anne, which added to the friction between her and her mother.

Winter weather brought other concerns. The government had rationed gas and electricity. Food was becoming scarce across the Netherlands.

This is no longer enough money for food ration coupons.

How much more do you need?

The families had saved money to use while in hiding. Mr. Kugler also secretly supplied money from Opekta. This paid for their food rations and anything else they needed.

The families often listened to the radio in the company's private office. They could only listen when there were no workers around. But in May, the government ordered radios to be turned in to punish people for acts of resistance. It also kept people from hearing reports about the war from Britain.

I'll find you another radio soon.

June 15, 1943
. . . the radio with its miraculous voice helps us to keep up our morale and to say again, 'chins up, stick it out, better times will come!

In June Mr. Voskuijl became ill. Opekta hired someone to replace him in the warehouse. Mr. van Pels lost his wallet there on a Monday morning in October.

My wallet has to be here. I had it when we came down earlier.

Are you sure?

Where exactly did you see it last?

They didn't know that the new employee, Mr. van Maaren, had found the wallet in the warehouse. He delivered it to the office—empty. It had contained the van Pels's only money. The wallet also made van Maaren suspicious.

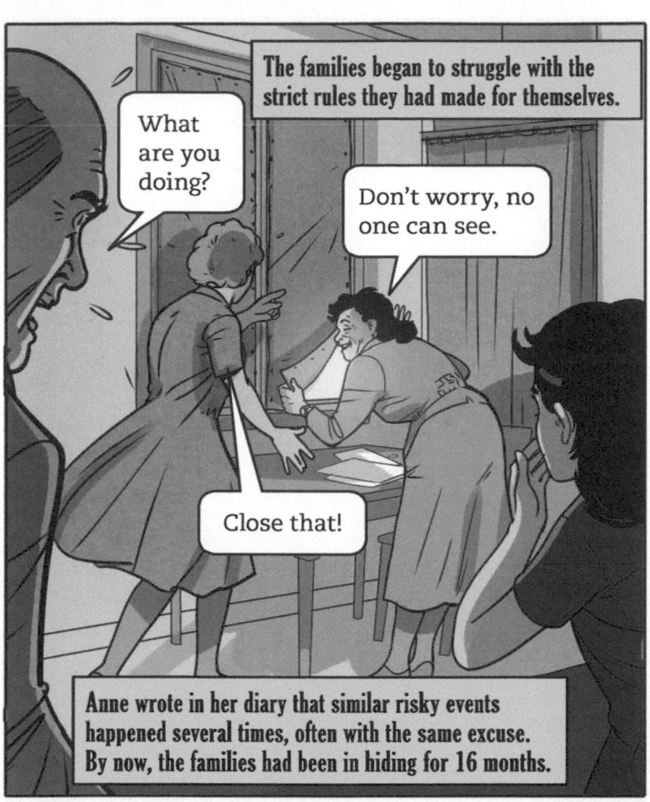
The families began to struggle with the strict rules they had made for themselves.
What are you doing?
Don't worry, no one can see.
Close that!
Anne wrote in her diary that similar risky events happened several times, often with the same excuse. By now, the families had been in hiding for 16 months.

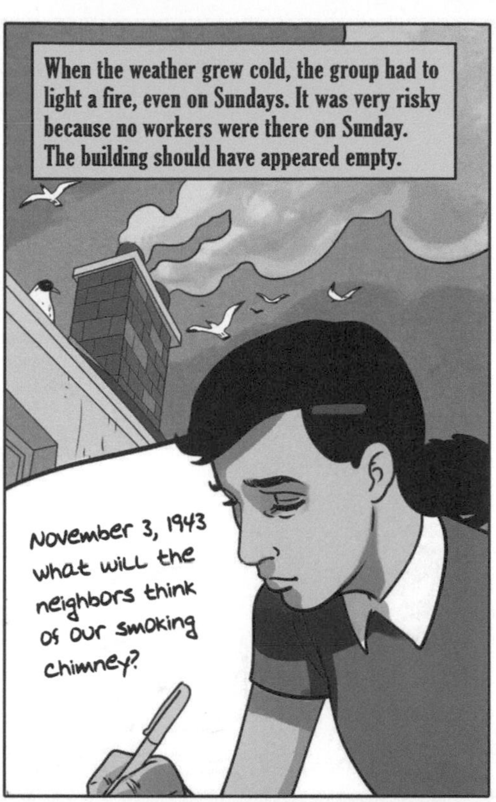
When the weather grew cold, the group had to light a fire, even on Sundays. It was very risky because no workers were there on Sunday. The building should have appeared empty.
November 3, 1943 what will the neighbors think of our smoking chimney?

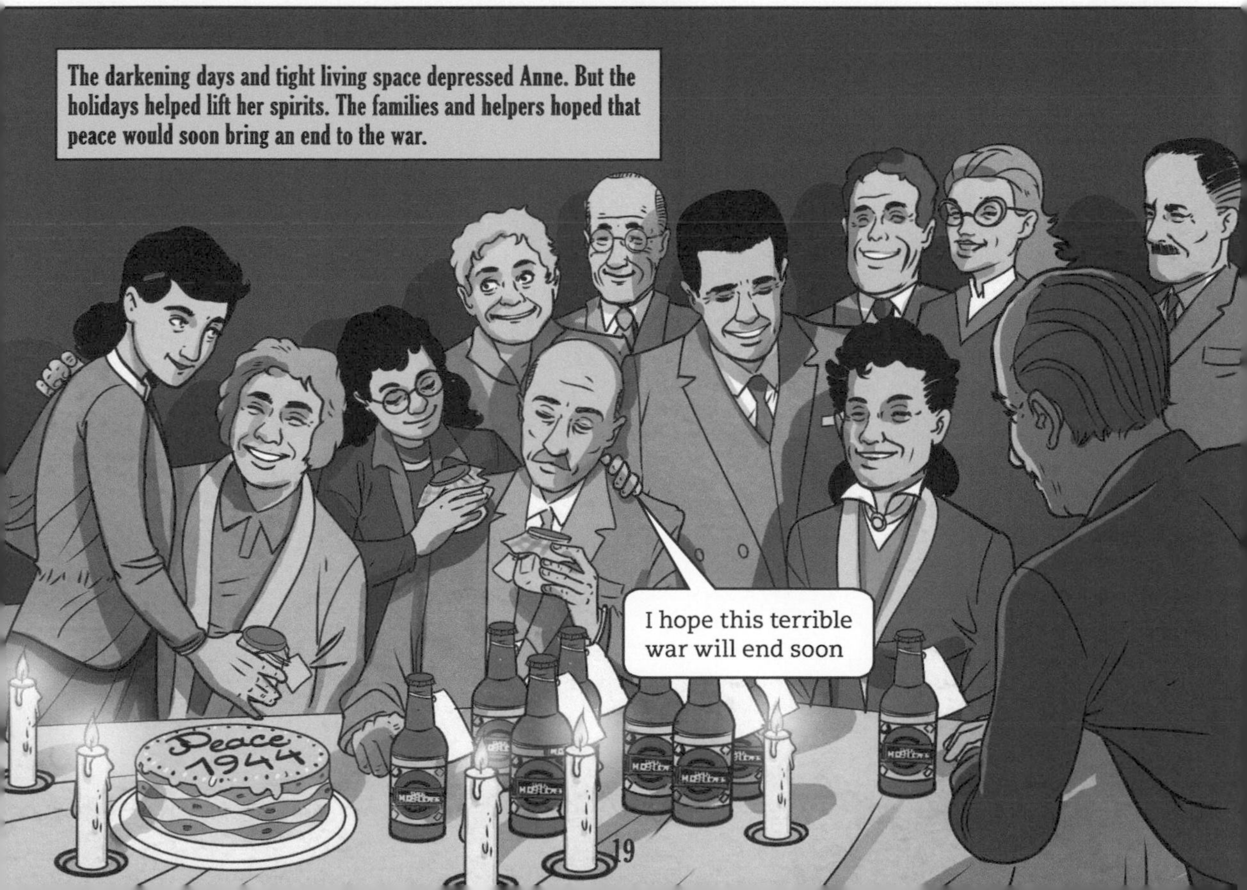
The darkening days and tight living space depressed Anne. But the holidays helped lift her spirits. The families and helpers hoped that peace would soon bring an end to the war.
I hope this terrible war will end soon
Peace 1944

1944

RATATATATATAT

RATATATATATA

RATATATATA

As Anne grew older, she knew she had changed. She argued less and slept in her own bed. She felt braver and more mature. She even walked downstairs in the dark by herself while German planes flew overhead.

Although Anne felt braver, the families still worried. The Allies were making progress, but adults thought that would make the Germans nervous. They thought the Nazis would flood the city to keep the British from winning it.

Is that possible?

Oh, yes. The Dutch have flooded the canals in the past to keep out invaders.

Another fear was that the Nazis would force everyone, both Jews and non-Jews, to leave.

They could march us all out of the city.

To trains and then camps.

We must invite our helpers here then.

Yes. We should store extra food just in case.

February 3, 1944
I trust to luck, but should I be saved ... then it would be terrible if my diaries and my tales were lost.

On February 29, Mr. van Pels discovered a mess in the office.

Has there been a burglar here?

He checked the front door, but it was locked. He guessed Bep had left the mess.

The following morning, Peter found the front door open.

What if the thief saw Mr. van Pels?

The mantel wasn't disturbed when I left last night. He must have been hiding in here.

There's nothing to do about it now.

Anne understood the importance of courage and faith. If the thief reported what he saw, police would come for them. But getting upset wouldn't change anything.

A month later, a radio broadcast urged people to keep journals as a record of living conditions under the Nazis.

That's what Anne is doing!

Really? Anne, let's have a look.

I'm writing it, but I'm not ready to show it yet.

Anne had decided to revise her diary. She hoped to publish it one day.

Anne wanted to become a journalist. She wrote short stories of life in the annex and even a novel. She hoped she had enough talent to be a successful writer after the war was over.

April 5, 1944: I can't imagine that I would have to lead the same sort of life as Mommy and Mrs. van Pels and all the women who do the work and are then forgotten. I must have something besides a husband and children...

Thieves broke into the building again on April 9, and a night guard contacted the police. An officer later began rattling the bookcase as they inspected the scene.

Now we are lost.

RUMBL RUMBLE

Thankfully, the bookcase kept their secret, but no one dared to move.

We must be brave like soldiers.

The next morning they risked a phone call to Mr. Kleiman. He promised to improve the building's security.

To improve their safety, Peter was given the job of bolting the building's door at night and unlocking it in the morning. But one day he forgot to unlock it, which made the company workers suspicious.

Let's try the window up there.

The windows above the kitchen were part of the annex. Thankfully, Mr. Kugler steered the workers away from them.

The kitchen window is a better option. Help me pry it open.

When potato flour went missing from their stored food, Otto and the others believed van Maaren was involved. But he had accused Bep of stealing it.

Van Maaren must have taken it himself. Why else accuse Bep?

So fire him.

We can't. If we do that, he may reveal what he suspects about us to the police.

You're right. You'll have to watch him closely.

Van Maaren's theft of their food made life difficult. Earlier, two people who sold them ration coupons had been arrested. One was their vegetable man, van Hoeven. This resulted in less food and more fear for the families.

GROENTEN & FRUITS
van Hoeven

May 25, 1944:
This morning V. Hoeven was picked up for having two Jews in his house. It is a great blow to us.

The families had to skip breakfast, and lunch was just porridge. Dinner was made up of rotting lettuce or spinach with potatoes and powdered gravy.

Ugh, even the bread is going rotten.

Meanwhile, they waited and listened for news of the Allies attacking Germany.

Enough about the Pacific. When will the Allies get here?

Perhaps they won't come.

Germany is too strong. The Allies can't win.

Anne ignored the constant disagreements about the war. Instead, she longed to go outside and go to school.

By early June, the Franks were nearly out of money.

How will we eat next month?

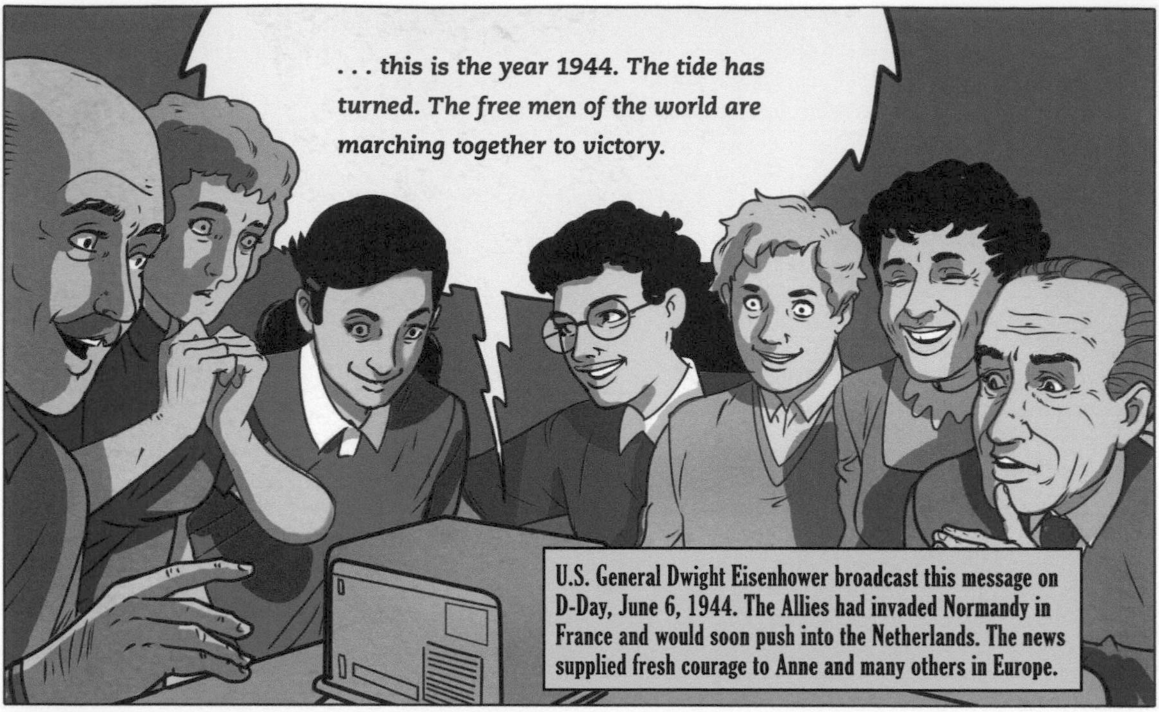

. . . this is the year 1944. The tide has turned. The free men of the world are marching together to victory.
U.S. General Dwight Eisenhower broadcast this message on D-Day, June 6, 1944. The Allies had invaded Normandy in France and would soon push into the Netherlands. The news supplied fresh courage to Anne and many others in Europe.

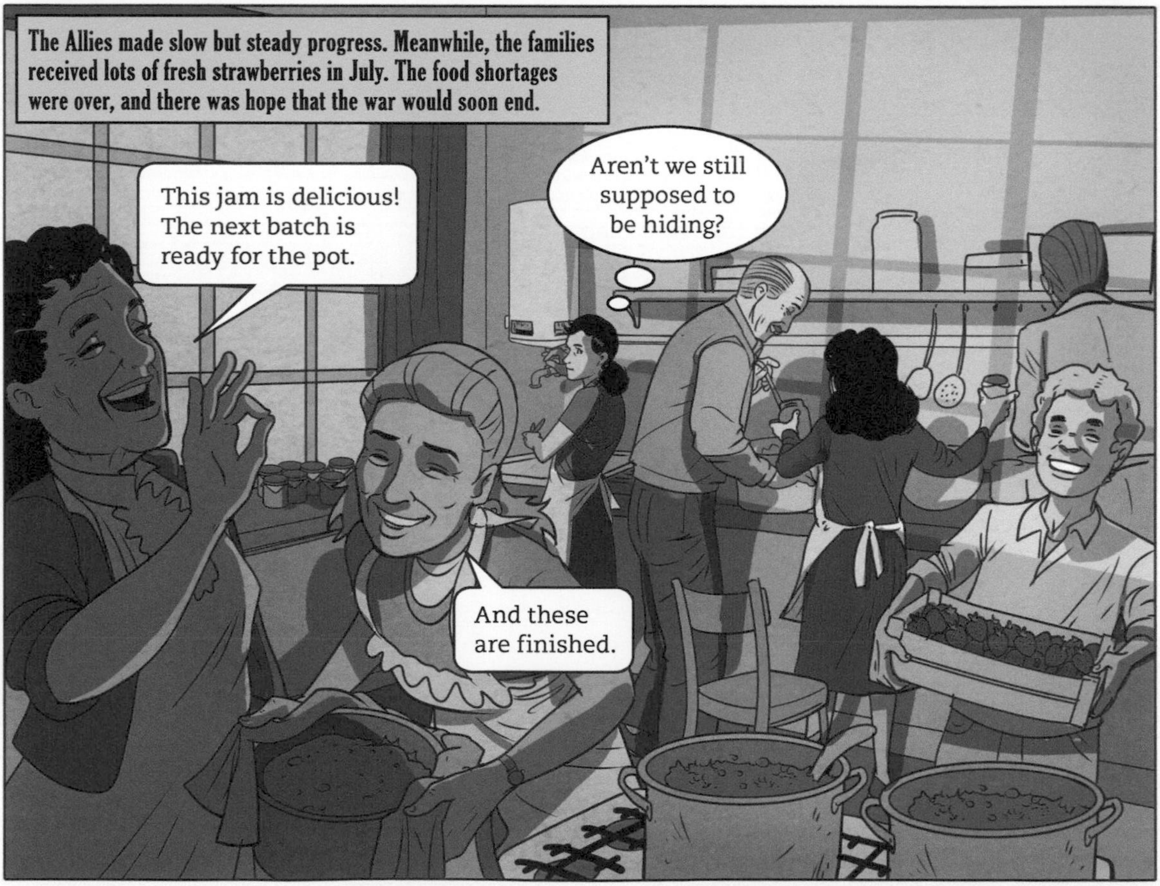

The Allies made slow but steady progress. Meanwhile, the families received lots of fresh strawberries in July. The food shortages were over, and there was hope that the war would soon end.
This jam is delicious! The next batch is ready for the pot.
Aren't we still supposed to be hiding?
And these are finished.

On August 4, 1944, armed men entered the offices to look for illegal goods or hidden Jews. Mr. Kugler knew that they'd search the whole building. He had to show them the annex.

Where are they?

What are you hiding here?

The hidden families were quickly discovered. The police lined the Jews up. All eight were brave as soldiers. They were taken to separate concentration camps in September, 1944. Anne and Margot stayed together.

Where is your money? Where are your valuables?

Mr. Kugler and Mr. Kleiman were also arrested, but Miep and Bep were not.

Miep and Bep discovered Anne's diary after the soldiers left. Miep locked it in her desk to keep it safe.

Years later, Anne's diary would be shared with the world so everyone could see the courage one young girl showed in the middle of the Holocaust.

ANNE'S LASTING LEGACY

In February 1945, while in the concentration camp, Anne and Margot both became seriously ill with typhus. The deadly disease was caused by the crowded and filthy conditions at the camp. Anne died a few days after Margot.

This is the legacy of your daughter, Anne.

Otto Frank was the only member of the hidden group to survive until the war ended. It took Otto a long time to read Anne's diary. Friends later convinced him to publish it. They told him it was a great history of the war and well written.

Anne's diary was published in 1947 in the Netherlands. Since then it has been translated into more than 70 languages.

There have also been many books, TV shows, movies, and plays based on Anne's story. Her short stories were published as the book *Tales from the Secret Annex.* Anne's work reminds the world of the Holocaust in the hope that similar horrors won't happen again.

The Franks' hiding place became a museum called Anne Frank House in 1957. There, visitors can learn more about Anne's life and experiences. The museum also provides materials and exhibits to teach people about the horrors of the Holocaust.

The duty Anne left me gives me strength. Will you help?

Of course, but what duty?

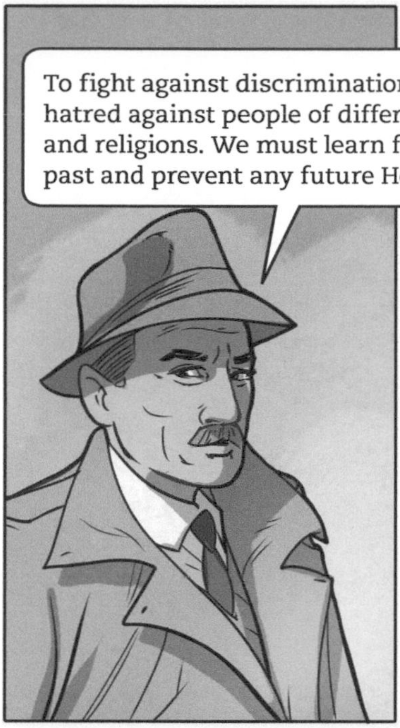
To fight against discrimination and hatred against people of different races and religions. We must learn from the past and prevent any future Holocaust.

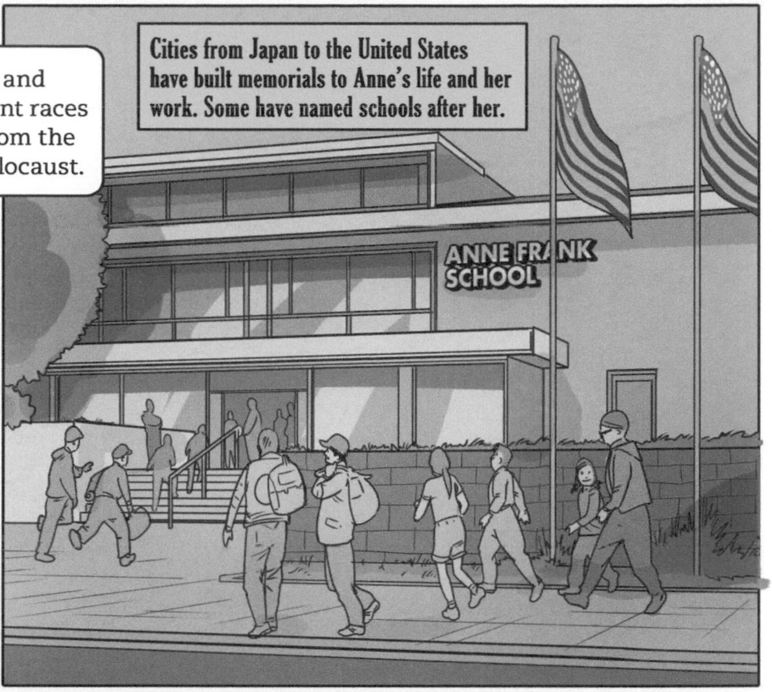
Cities from Japan to the United States have built memorials to Anne's life and her work. Some have named schools after her.
ANNE FRANK SCHOOL

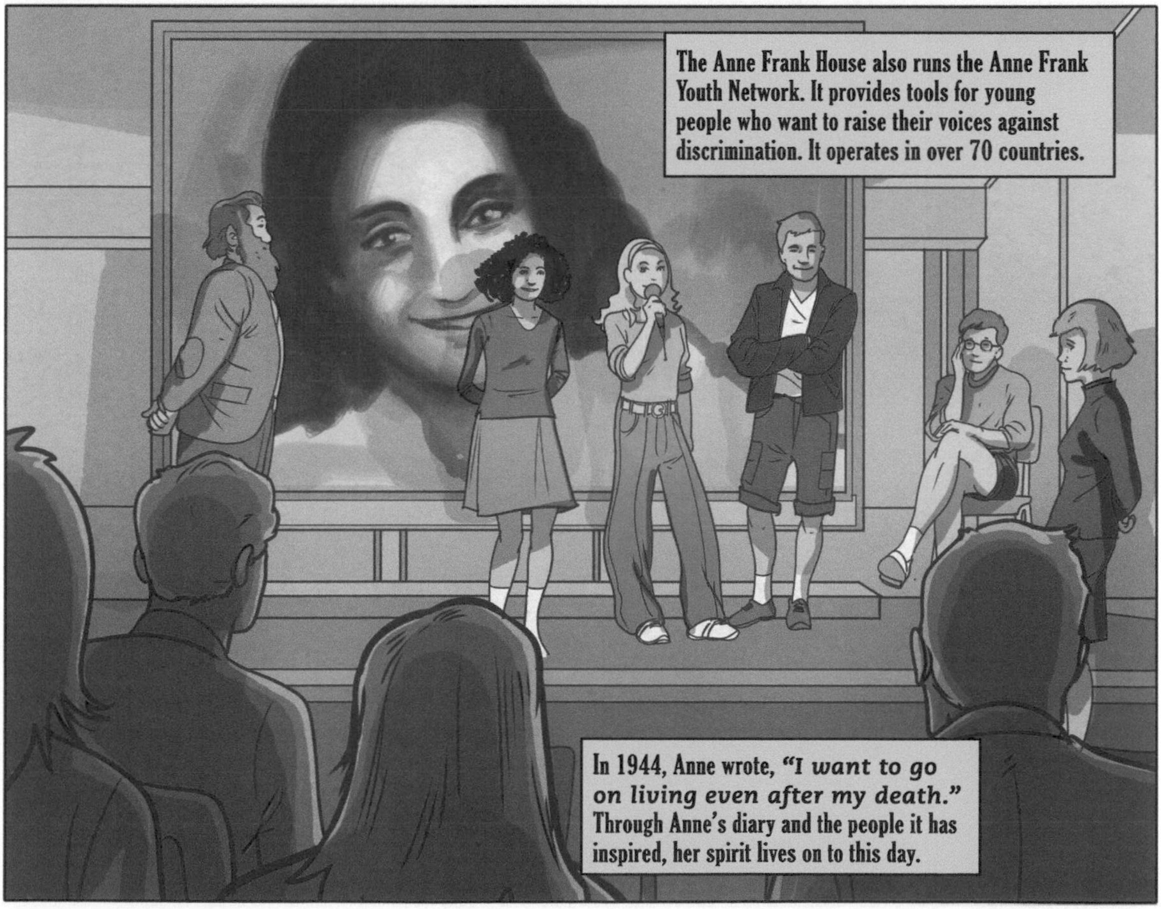
The Anne Frank House also runs the Anne Frank Youth Network. It provides tools for young people who want to raise their voices against discrimination. It operates in over 70 countries.
In 1944, Anne wrote, *"I want to go on living even after my death."* Through Anne's diary and the people it has inspired, her spirit lives on to this day.

GLOSSARY

Allies (AL-eyes)—a group of countries that fought together in World War II, including the United States, England, France, and the Soviet Union

anti-Semitic (an-tie-SEM-eh-tik)—discrimination and hatred of Jewish people because of their culture, religion, or race

concentration camp (kahn-suhn-TRAY-shuhn KAMP)—a camp where people such as prisoners of war, political prisoners, or refugees are held; usually referring to locations in Germany during World War II where Jews were killed in large numbers

discrimination (dis-kri-muh-NAY-shuhn)—treating people unfairly because of their race, gender, religion, or country of birth

Holocaust (HAH-luh-kost)—the mass murder of millions of Jewish people, gay people, and other groups by the Nazis during World War II

Nazi Party (NOT-see PAR-tee)—the German political party led by Adolf Hitler that controlled Germany from 1939 to 1945

refugee (ref-yuh-JEE)—a person who has to leave a place to escape war or other disasters

segregate (SEG-ruh-gayt)—to keep people of different races apart in school and other public places

READ MORE

Berne, Emma Carson. *The Story of Anne Frank*. Emeryville, CA: Rockridge Press, 2021.

Lowell, Barbara. *Behind the Bookcase: Miep Gies, Anne Frank, and the Hiding Place*. Minneapolis: Kar-Ben Publishing, an imprint of Lerner Publishing, 2020.

Radomski, Kassandra. *Anne Frank: Get to Know the Girl Beyond Her Diary*. North Mankato, MN: Capstone Press, 2019.

INTERNET SITES

Anne Frank
biography.com/activist/anne-frank

Anne Frank: Her Life, the Diary, and the Secret Annex
annefrank.org/en/anne-frank/

Biography: Anne Frank
ducksters.com/biography/women_leaders/anne_frank.php

INDEX

Anne Frank House, 28, 29
anti-Semitism, 4–5, 8–9, 15

Eisenhower, Dwight, 26

food, 18, 21, 24, 25, 26
Frank, Anne, 5
  birth of, 6
  death of, 28
  diary, 9, 11, 12, 13, 15, 17, 18, 19, 21,
    22, 24, 27, 28–29
  legacy of, 28–29
Frank, Edith, 5, 6, 9, 14, 17
Frank, Margot, 5, 6, 9, 10, 13, 14, 17,
    27, 28
Frank, Otto, 5, 6, 9, 14, 16, 28

helpers, 6, 8, 11, 13, 15, 18, 19, 21, 23,
    24, 27
Hitler, Adolf, 4, 5, 7, 8
Holocaust, 7, 27, 28, 29
  concentration camps, 5, 7, 21, 27, 28

Nazis, 4, 5, 6, 7, 8, 17, 20, 21, 22
Netherlands, 6, 7, 8, 18, 26, 28

Opekta, 6, 8, 13, 18

Pfeffer, Fritz, 17

radios, 18, 22
refugees, 7, 8

Secret Annex, 10, 11, 28
  arguments, 14, 25
  celebrating holidays, 15, 19
  close calls, 16, 22, 23
  daily life, 12–13, 15
  discovery of, 27
  hidden entrance, 11, 16, 22, 23
  rules of, 17, 19

van Maaren, 18, 24
van Pels family, 9, 10, 14, 18, 21

World War I, 4, 8
World War II, 8, 16, 18, 19, 25, 26, 28
  Allies, 16, 20, 25, 26

ABOUT THE AUTHOR

Renaissance Studio, Ltd

Debbie Vilardi is a freelance editor and author of over 20 leveled readers, poems, short stories, and personal essays for children and adults. Her most recent publication, "Aunt Esther's Coat" (*Mishpacha, Jr.*, Issue 835, 2020), has Jewish themes and is based on her family's history in New York City during the depression. Debbie lives on Long Island with her husband and two teens.